INVENTORS & INVENTIONS

LASERS

INVENTORS & INVENTIONS

LASERS

MARY VIRGINIA FOX

BENCHMARK BOOKS

MARSHALL CAVENDISH
NEW YORK

Benchmark Books
Marshall Cavendish Corporation
99 White Plains Road
Tarrytown, New York 10591-9001

©Marshall Cavendish Corporation, 1996

Series created by The Creative Publishing Company

Library of Congress Cataloging-in-Publication Data

Fox, Mary Virginia.
    Lasers / Mary Virginia Fox.
        p.   cm. -- (Inventors & inventions)
    Includes bibliographical references & index.
    Summary: Describes the discovery, principles, and types of lasers,
the light they produce, their contributions to industry, medicine,
war, crime detection, communication, and other fields--and future
uses of their amazing powers.
    ISBN 0-7614-0067-2
    1. Lasers--Juvenile literature.   [1. Lasers.]   I. Title.
II. Series.
TA1682.F68   1996
621.36'6--dc20

95-9098
CIP
AC

Printed and bound in Hong Kong

Acknowledgments

Technical Consultant: Steven L. Barnicki, Ph.D.
Illustrations on pages 11, 13, and 43 by Julian Baker

The publishers would like to thank the following for their permission to reproduce photographs:
Dr. R. Menzel, (40, 41); Photo Press Defence Pictures, (J. Flack 35); Dr. P. Piironen, (30); Science Photo Library
Ltd, (Jim Amos 21, BSIP, Laurent 59, Martin Dohrn 50, Gordon Garradd 10, Alexander Isiaras 8,
Lawrence Livermore National Laboratory/University of California 58, Los Alamos National Laboratory 31,
Tim Malyon 51, Jerry Mason 54, Will & Deni McIntyre 57, NASA 24, 25, 28, Joseph Nettis 7, Alfred Pasieka 52,
Philippe Plailly frontispiece, 26, 42, 44, 45, 53, Santa Fe Technologies Inc. 32, U.S. Department of Energy
front cover, Erik Viktor 38, John Walsh 48); Science & Society Picture Library, 16, 47); Dr. G. Sterken, (56);
UPI/Bettmann, (14, 15, 18, 19, 20, 22, 23, 36, 44, 55).

(Cover) A scientist uses an argon-ion laser to analyze the flow of coal ash particles in exhaust gases.

(Frontispiece) A hologram, on film and illuminated by halogen lamp, of the Palace of Discovery in Paris.

Contents

── Chapter 1 ──
A Ray of Hope

Death was near. The patient was weak and in pain. A team of doctors had been consulted, but no treatment seemed safe in this particular case. All agreed that the patient's main arteries had become so clogged that life-giving blood and oxygen were not circulating well through his body.

Major surgery to remove the block and repair arteries would require too long a time under anesthetic for the patient's weakened condition. Another simpler technique might be to insert a tiny balloon into the blood vessel. By inflating it and compressing the plaque that was stopping the blood flow, the artery might be cleared, but the result could be fatal. If the plaque broke away and rushed through the patient's vascular system on its way to the brain, a stroke could easily be the result.

A third untried procedure was suggested by Dr. Milton Flocks at Stanford University Medical Center — a laser beam. Dr. Flocks and his associate, Dr. Christian Zweng, had been studying promising reports from laboratory procedures. The equipment was available. It was worth a try.

A thin optical fiber was inserted into the blood vessel to give the doctor a clear view of what had to be done. A small camera at the end of the fiber took pictures of the blockage in the artery. Then, the instrument directing the laser was inserted through a small incision, and the miraculous beam of light concentrated to the thickness of a strand of hair was able to cut a clean line all around the hardened matter, instantly vaporizing the plaque.

The procedure had taken only seconds, but when the minor operation was over, the patient's blood flow was restored to

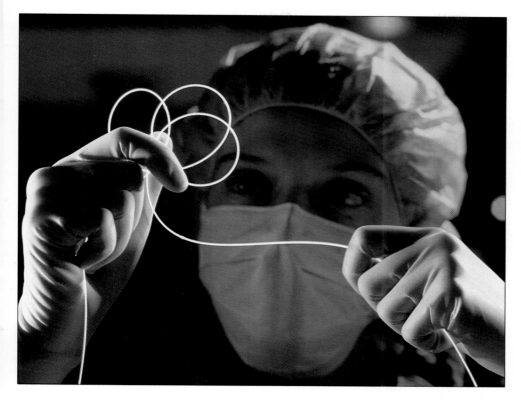

A surgeon holds a bundle of optical fibers. They will be inserted into the patient's blood vessels and transmit a laser beam that will clear the arteries of plaque. Today, lasers make it easier to perform surgical operations that once were considered too dangerous.

normal, and his strength returned. The year was 1963. Since then this radical but simple technique has proved successful in hundreds of cases.

Seeing Is Believing

Because laser light is one pure color and of a single wavelength, it will be absorbed only by certain colors, depending on the type of the laser beam. In other words, a laser is able to select its target.

An amusing experiment demonstrating one of the laser's characteristics caught the attention of many doctors. A blue balloon was inflated inside a transparent one. When the ruby red beam of a special laser was aimed at the double balloon, only the blue one exploded. The outer one remained intact.

In eye surgery, this is exactly what happens. Eyes are covered with an outer transparent envelope called the cornea and backed by the dark-colored blood-webbed retina. It is very difficult

AMAZING FACTS

Using carbon dioxide, the CO_2 laser operates in the infrared wavelength, producing an invisible ray. A red light directs the surgeon's hand when it is used as a scalpel. The CO_2 laser scalpel cuts by heating the water in cells extremely rapidly, turning it into steam. The laser beam also seals small capillary blood vessels as it cuts by cauterizing them, reducing the need for clamping off blood vessels during surgery.

during ordinary surgery to reach this hidden area without causing damage to other parts of the eye.

Surgeons found that a laser could be used to spot-weld detached retinas. Firing the beam, they saw that it passed harmlessly through the patient's cornea and affected only the small area that needed to be touched, just as the laser beam had passed through the transparent balloon and exploded the colored balloon inside the larger clear covering.

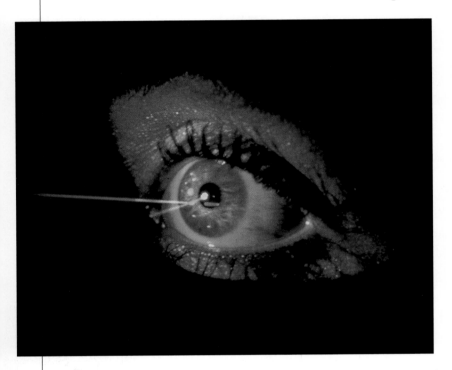

The red beam of a helium-neon laser passes through the pupil of a human eye. Since this technology was introduced, eye surgery has become much safer. Only those parts of the eye that need treatment are touched.

People who have diabetes often face blindness; weakened blood vessels leak blood into the interior of the eye and obscure their vision. Because they can make such a small pit, lasers can cauterize the blood vessel, sealing it off to stop it from seeping blood into the clear fluid of the eye. Glaucoma and cataract surgery is also much safer now. Nearsightedness can be treated by a skilled ophthalmologist, an eye specialist, who can shape the very curve of the eye's lens to fix an individual's vision.

Fixing Ears, Teeth, and Skin

Even a type of hearing loss can be treated with lasers. The stapes bone is one of a series of bones that transmit vibrations to the inner ear and help us to hear. Hardening of the arteries can cause the stapes bone to lock in place, completely blocking sound. Previously, surgeons had to use tiny picks and chisels to free the stapes. The new procedure, using a laser beam, avoids damaging surrounding tissue and reduces bleeding.

Dentists are able to zap out decay within a tooth without that awful drill, and excellent progress has been made in the use of low-powered lasers to harden tooth enamel. One day, we may have teeth that last a lifetime.

Some people are born with disfiguring birthmarks. Others may, in the enthusiasm of the moment, have chosen to mark their skin with lasting tattoos. Today, it is possible to change the surface of the skin, in most cases without the scars that had once been the result of deeper surgery.

What Else Can a Laser Do?

These examples show the delicate uses of lasers, but this magic beam can cut through substances as hard as steel and diamonds. Used to make three-dimensional photographs called holograms, lasers can also guide missiles and shell targets. They can record and play back music. At the grocery store, lasers read the code on packages that tell the price of an item. Laser printers are in use all over the world, and our communication system has been revolutionized by the ability of lasers to carry our messages over networks. Lasers can pierce clouds and send back messages that help us determine cycles of weather. Our entire fingerprinting system depends on the reliability of laser measurements in the crime lab.

A steel plate is cut by an infrared laser as part of a program testing smaller and more powerful lasers in the auto industry.

Nuclear fusion caused by a laser may someday solve energy problems. There seems no limit to the use of lasers, and yet they are one of our newest discoveries.

We see rainbows when sunlight is refracted by water in the sky. Ordinary white light, what we think of as daylight, breaks up into its component colors by spreading out its different wavelengths. This allows the human eye to see at least seven different colors.

Light as Energy

It seems strange that something as common as light had not been developed into an exact science long ago. Scientists had been piecing together some facts that helped the early pioneers in laser research, but the whole picture was unclear.

By the early 1800s, it was established that light, while traveling essentially in straight lines, is produced in waves, like the waves in water. And like water waves, light comes in different *wavelengths*, measured from one crest to another as a wave passes a given point. The waves also come in different heights, or *amplitudes*, measured from crest to trough. Light waves are also measured by their *frequencies*, meaning the number of waves that pass a specific point during a certain amount of time. In the late 1800s, German physicist Max Planck showed that, besides traveling in waves, light also comes in precise particles of energy or *photons*, particles that could be forced to behave in certain ways.

A Rainbow of Colors

Ordinary white light is really a mixture of all colors. Before or after a storm, when there are many small particles of water in the sky to refract the light, sunlight may break up into a rainbow of colors. Sunlight also contains a broad range of electromagnetic radiation, from radio waves through the entire visible range of colors to

ultraviolet waves we cannot see. Electric light, candlelight, and moonlight are all soupy collections of photons varying in many different proportions.

Laser light is made up of a collection of identical photons, each exactly like the other. Thus, the light from a laser is a very special kind of concentrated light with exactly one color and frequency and one measurement of wavelength. Photons of light that "stick together" and travel together form the laser beam. This does not happen in nature; scientists had to invent a way to make this happen.

Visible light is part of a much larger electromagnetic spectrum. It merges into infrared waves at longer wavelengths and into ultraviolet waves at shorter wavelengths. At more extreme wavelengths and frequencies are other types of electromagnetic radiation that we often use in today's technology.

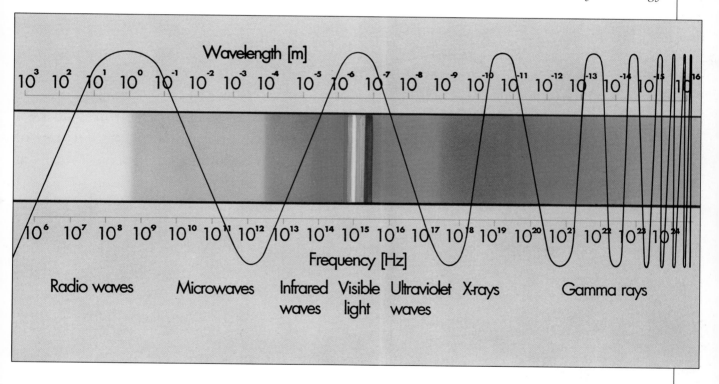

What Does the Word Mean?

The word *laser* stands for the phrase *light amplification by stimulated emission of radiation*. Despite the phrasing, it really isn't all that complicated to understand the process. The difficulty came in manufacturing a "gadget" that would prove that light could be concentrated in such a way.

Before there were lasers, Charles H. Townes invented what was called the *maser*, using microwaves instead of light waves. Townes did not set out to invent the laser but to produce very high frequency radio waves, or microwaves. He hoped these tiny waves of energy would be able to probe the very essence of matter — to explore atoms, their nuclei, and electrons. What he was trying to do was to make a series of microwaves all behave the same.

Think of a crowd of people all doing the wave at a football game. It all starts with just one or two people who stand up, a mere ripple of movement. But as more and more people join the crowd action, what started out as a single person waving in the stadium turns into a powerful force all flowing in one direction.

Instead of a stadium full of people, think of an atom with electrons swirling around a nucleus. These electrons may occupy higher or lower levels of energy. Most of the time, electrons are said to be in the *ground* or *low state*. When an electron is hit by a photon, or light particle of energy, it jumps up to a higher state of energy. The atom is then said to be in an excited state. Atoms in a laser are excited from the energy being pumped into it.

The excited state resulting from the bump from the photon only lasts for a fraction of a second. Then, the electron drops down to where it was originally. As it drops, the atom loses this added bit of energy, dropping off the photon as a particle of light of the same wavelength and frequency as the particle that bombarded it in the first place. Now there are two photons, the original one and the new one.

They go off in exactly the same direction and are exactly alike. It's like bouncing a ball off a wall, but instead of one ball coming back, you get two, moving in exactly the same direction. When one of these two photons (or balls) passes near a neighboring excited atom and stimulates it, a third photon is released. This chain reaction results in a lot of light that is all of one frequency and wavelength. In other words, bombarding atoms with photons will stimulate them to emit light. This is called stimulated emission of radiation, the *s-e-r* in the word *laser*.

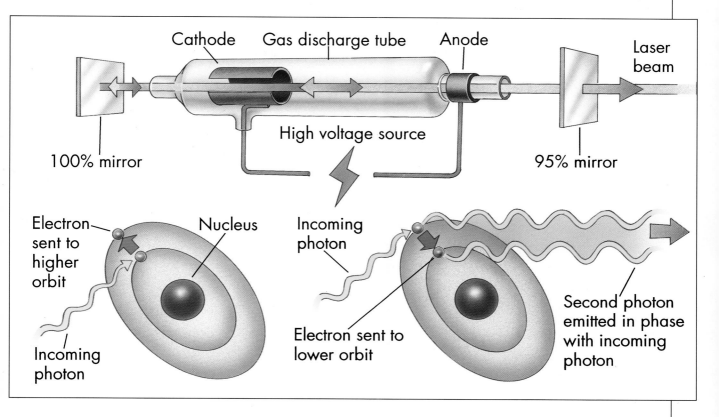

Cathode   Gas discharge tube   Anode   Laser beam

High voltage source

100% mirror

95% mirror

Electron sent to higher orbit

Nucleus

Incoming photon

Incoming photon

Electron sent to lower orbit

Second photon emitted in phase with incoming photon

The Origins of the Maser and the Laser

Charles Townes discovered the basic principle of a maser while studying ammonia molecules in 1951. But while a laser emits visible light, a maser produces microwaves, whose wavelengths are longer than visible light and thus invisible. One problem with the first masers was that a great many atoms had to be kept in the excited state while the beam was being focused. The maser had to be pumped with energy after every burst.

So who was the first to invent the laser itself? The answer has all the melodrama of a good mystery. Millions of dollars are at stake in sorting out the rights to patents for lasers, the right to make, use, and sell an invention. Intense rivalry has been seething for the past four decades between at least three brilliant contenders for the honor: Charles Hard Townes, Thomas Harold Maiman, and Gordon Gould.

Laser light builds up in a tube with mirrors at both ends so that it reflects from one end to the other. It is allowed to escape in small quantities from one end to form a laser beam. Laser light is created when a photon hits another atom and starts a chain reaction that causes more photons to be emitted, all of one frequency and wavelength.

Charles Hard Townes

Charles Hard Townes was born July 28, 1915, in Greenville, South Carolina. His father was a well-respected attorney in the town, but Charles's interests were in other fields. He studied modern languages and physics at Furman University in Greenville. At one time, he thought of becoming a physician, but in his sophomore year, he switched to physics.

Townes had a year of graduate work at Duke University and was then advised that groundbreaking research was being performed at the California Institute of Technology. He became interested in searching for radio waves in interstellar space and was the first to discover molecules in space consisting of elements with complicated atomic structures.

He received his Ph.D. in physics in 1939 and was immediately offered a job at the Bell Telephone Laboratories. His real work was just beginning.

The first confirmed date of a real breakthrough in the invention of lasers and masers came on the morning of April 26, 1951. In town for a scientific conference, Charles Townes was sitting on a park bench enjoying a beautiful spring day in Washington, D.C. The idea seemed to come to him in a blinding flash of light, and he scribbled his idea on the back of an envelope.

Townes did not discuss the new idea with committee

members at the scientific meeting, but he did not keep his idea a secret. He waited until he got back to his laboratory at Columbia University to share the theory he hoped someone would be able to prove. He challenged the scientific world to come up with a working model using his theory.

By 1954, Townes was able to separate the unexcited atoms in ammonia gas from the excited atoms, which gave off a concentrated microwave beam when they dropped back to their original state. The atoms of gas were being used as amplifiers — duplicators of the excited atoms. The concept paved the way for new developments; the laser was soon to follow.

Charles Townes, left, and a colleague, Dr. J. P. Gordon, with the first maser.

Townes was very well known in scientific circles, but he was never one to take his prestige seriously. He was once asked how to define the real purpose of his maser. In jest, he took the letters of the word maser and gave it a new meaning — *m*ethod for *a*ttaining *s*cientific *e*xpensive *r*esearch.

In 1959, Dr. Townes took a leave of absence to serve as a director with the Department of Defense, where he was concerned with problems of national defense and foreign policy. He was also asked to advise NASA (the National Aeronautics and Space Administration) on research planned for the Apollo lunar landings.

In 1964, Townes received the Nobel Prize in physics for his work in studying the smallest particles of energy yet isolated by maser equipment. Maser development in the decade that followed Townes's original ammonia device was rapid, creating the field of research and technology known as quantum electronics. He was a brilliant scientist who led the way for many new ways to study basic elements on Earth and in space.

— Chapter 2 —
The Challenge Is Met

In 1958, Townes and his brother-in-law, Arthur Schawlow, collaborated on an article in a scientific journal describing just how a laser should work and challenged anyone to build it. Many tried but failed.

Theodore Harold Maiman accepted the challenge and succeeded. Most scientists thought that a laser would eventually be made by passing an electric current through a gas. But Maiman, working alone at the Hughes Research Laboratories in Malibu, California, started by using a small rod of synthetic ruby about one and one-half inches (four centimeters) long. He had to use a synthetic ruby because a real ruby would have had too many imperfections.

Maiman then surrounded the rod with a spiral-shaped flash lamp, similar to flash lamps used in cameras. The intense light of the flash excited the chromium atoms of the ruby to jump to a high level. When the atoms at this level quickly dropped down to their lower normal level, they released photons of light. When these photons of light stimulated other excited chromium atoms, they produced more photons that were exact copies of the ones that had excited them.

An early ruby laser consisted of a polished ruby crystal coated with silver at both ends to form mirrors that reflected the light back and forth through the rod. A small opening at one end allowed the laser light to escape in pulses.

Simply left to itself, a stimulated ruby rod would not form a beam, but just a red glow. Amplification was needed. Maiman polished both ends of the ruby rod and coated them with silver, like the backing of a mirror, so that they would reflect the light back into the ruby. Stimulated emissions that leaked out from the side of the rod were lost, but the light that was reflected back into the length of the ruby grew in intensity. One photon became two and two became four and so on. Only a very small opening in one mirror at the end of a rod was left through which a beam of light could pass. The laser light is deliberately leaked out through that tiny hole.

A laser beam is concentrated, not like the beam of a flashlight that spreads from its source to illuminate a whole room. This happens because the light waves of a laser are parallel, clones of each other. In step with each other, they produce light of the same frequency.

The First Time

The first flash from Maiman's laser lasted only three hundred-millionths of a second, but it was the very first time anyone had ever been able to amplify a light beam. Scientists had been able to amplify microwaves, radio waves, and electrical signals. They also had been able to generate light but never to add energy to it. The atoms in the ruby were behaving like billions of tiny light amplifiers, and what they were amplifying was measured in staggering quantities.

Scientists measure energy, which is related to brightness, in several different ways. Power is measured in *watts*. This represents how much energy is radiated, but brightness alone does not describe the work energy can do. A candle is not very bright. You can pass your hand right through the flame of a candle without burning your skin, so long as you do it rapidly enough, but if you hold your hand over the flame for some time, it can cause painful burns.

AMAZING FACTS

Ordinary light spreads quickly as its waves travel off in different, ever-widening, directions. The waves of laser light travel in the same direction. They spread so little that when scientists fired a laser at the Moon through a telescope, the beam widened to only two miles (3.2 kilometers) in the quarter-million-mile (400,000 kilometer) journey.

Theodore Harold Maiman

Theodore Harold Maiman found fame suddenly, but hours of painstaking research had preceded his victory. That thorough research was a habit he had learned early in his life. He was guided into the world of science by his father, a creative electrical engineer who developed an innovative improvement in the efficiency of automobile engines.

Theodore Maiman was born July 11, 1927. As a teenager, rather than earning money cutting grass or serving food at the local restaurant, he saved up enough cash to pay for his first four years of college by repairing electrical appliances and radios.

There was no doubt in his mind that he wanted to study in the field of science. He graduated from the University of Colorado, earning his B.S. degree in engineering physics in 1949. His graduate work took him to Stanford University.

For his doctoral thesis, he studied the measurements of certain gases with a spectroscope. This instrument can pry information from the very center of elements by seeing how the energy waves of an element are splintered into lines of color through a prism. Maiman was very familiar with the microwave optical techniques used by Charles Townes and his associates.

However, Maiman was working alone when he did his maser and laser experiments during the time he was employed by

Theodore Maiman with a cube-shaped ruby crystal.

President Lyndon B. Johnson presents awards to Theodore Maiman, left, and Dr. Ali Javan, right, for their part in developing the laser beam. The little girl is Dr. Maiman's daughter, Sheri.

Hughes Research Laboratories. When his final breakthrough came with the use of the ruby laser, he formed his own company, Konrad Corporation, which became the leader in research and manufacture of high-powered lasers.

After Konrad was purchased by Union Carbide Corporation in 1968, he formed Maiman Associates, where he was a principal consultant in areas of lasers and optics. He was also involved in designing new systems for the Indak Corporation, where he directed the development of communication systems.

In 1972, he was a cofounder of Laser Video Corporation, where he was responsible for introducing large-screen laser-driven color video displays. By 1976, he was vice president for advanced technology at TRW Electronics.

He has received many international awards for his work in putting laser technology to practical use. Others can lay claim to having led the way in pushing science toward lasers, but it was Maiman who was the first to prove it could be done.

Why did Theodore Harold Maiman succeed when so many others had failed? The answer is simple according to Alan Mauer, science writer. "He tried harder."

Energy is measured in power (brightness in the case of light) multiplied by time (how long it radiates). One watt of power radiated for one second is known as a *joule*.

One-thousandth of a second after Maiman turned on the two thousand-joule flash lamp, pulses of red light streamed from the laser. Each bolt lasted one-millionth of a second, and in two-thousandths of a second, the entire process was over.

That tiny parcel of time was enough for something amazing to happen. At peak power, the spikes of this laser light radiated thirty thousand watts in a one square-centimeter beam. The Sun radiates only seven thousand watts per square centimeter at its surface. Harnessing such energy was mind-boggling, even to the scientists who had been working in the field.

The date was July 10, 1960. Maiman told the world that to generate a light wave as intense as that produced by a laser, a carbon-arc Hollywood klieg light, the brightest light produced till then, would have to reach a temperature of several billion degrees. Of course, the lamp would melt long before that would happen. Front-page stories in newspapers called it a death ray.

Actually, ruby lasers were not very practical since they emitted one quick pulse at a time, not long enough to do any real work. But lasers made of gas were soon to follow. They worked on exactly the same principal as crystal lasers but could remain on indefinitely, producing continuous beams.

Claiming to Be First

Although no one could dispute the fact that Theodore Maiman was the first to make an operational laser, there was one other person in the scramble for fame

Scientists in this 1967 picture measure the diffused beam of an argon-gas laser that NASA planned to use in Earth-to-space tracking and communication experiments.

A laser rod is manufactured. A mixture of yttrium-aluminum-garnet (YAG) and trace amounts of neodymium is heated in a crucible. Over the next twenty days, a single crystal will grow in the center of the crucible. It is then shaped and polished.

— Gordon Gould. As a graduate student in the physics department at Columbia University, his lab was just a few doors down the hall from Townes.

Gould was obsessed with the idea of developing a device that would concentrate light, rather than the microwaves Townes had worked with. He was unable to convince his professor to approve the project for his Ph.D. thesis, so he decided to go ahead alone.

In November of 1957, just two months after Townes revealed his design for what was then called an optical maser, Gould put down in his notebook his own ideas of how to build such a device. Gould was the first one to coin the word *laser*.

What Gould wrote was in contradiction to earlier laws stating that the temperature of a surface heated by a source of radiation could not exceed the temperature of the source. In practice, a laser operating at room temperature is capable of producing a beam that can melt steel. Was anyone ready to believe this?

Gould also saw that to amplify light, it would have to be pumped back and forth in a confined space. These were all

Gordon Gould is still fighting for recognition of the theories he developed in the 1950s about how lasers could be made to work.

important ideas he recorded, but instead of publishing them in scientific journals where they would be on record for everyone to see, he kept them to himself. He did have them notarized, as it happened, at a candy store close to his laboratory, so that he could prove the date when these ideas had been created in his own mind.

He realized that it would be important to protect his ideas, so he went to a lawyer who gave him incorrect advice. He was told that to be granted a patent he would have to have a working model. This was not true, but, believing this, he naively gave up the patenting process for the time.

Other Claims

The legal battle was about to begin. Charles Townes and Arthur Schawlow took their laser ideas to the patent office and obtained rights to the idea. Nine months later, Gould did file to patent similar ideas, giving as proof that his ideas were original, the notarized journal.

The case has been in the courts ever since. Gould left Columbia University without receiving his doctorate and took his idea to TRG, Inc., a small company in Syosset, New York, that was doing work for the military. The Defense Department was so impressed with the concept of the laser's heating effects that a million dollars was set aside for research. A tight security lid was put on the work carried on at TRG.

During the height of the cold war, when the United States and the Soviet Union were aiming weapons at each other, everyone connected with a military project was given a close security check. At that time in our history, there was a fear that Communist sympathizers might sabotage our democratic form of government. Anyone associated, even distantly or briefly, with communism was suspect.

Back in the early 1940s, Gould had married a young woman who announced that she was a Communist. Together they attended a Marxist study group. Gould's interest in socialism and communism ended in disillusionment in 1948 when the Soviet Union took over Czechoslovakia. His wife did not share his more conservative ideas, and they were divorced. But suspicions about his loyalty to his country caused by his early study of communism came to the surface just at the time he was busy with defense work. He was not allowed to work on his own project.

By a series of unfortunate events, Gordon Gould was denied what he claimed was his rightful place in history. He did win a limited victory in 1977 by obtaining two patents, one for laser pumping and the other for processing certain materials with lasers, but he is still fighting for patents that could earn him a fortune.

A student at Stanford University in 1968 adjusts the crystal, lens, and mirror system of the first laser to generate continuous visible laser light at varying wavelengths.

— Chapter 3 —
A New Way to Measure

The Hubble Space Telescope being deployed from the space shuttle Discovery *in April 1990. Lasers helped cutting machines measure the telescope's lenses and mirrors.*

One of the first uses of lasers was as a measuring tool. A light beam that would not sag or spread as it focused on objects was exactly what surveyors, engineers, and scientists

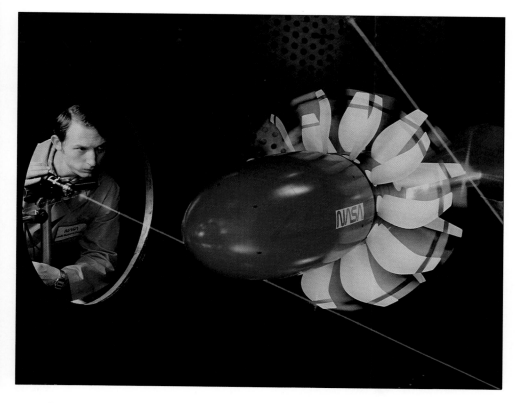

Testing a fan in a supersonic wind tunnel at the NASA Lewis Research Center. A laser can measure the deflection of the moving blades more accurately than any other method.

needed. Extremely delicate measurements were now possible as well as sightings in space.

Lasers have helped measure precise cutting machines that form optical lenses, both for the smallest microscope work and huge mirrors and lenses for astronomers' telescopes. The faulty lens of the Hubble Space Telescope, which is circling Earth on a satellite, was not caused by the equipment but by human error in not programming the polishing of the mirror correctly. The final error was less than the thickness of a human hair, a measurement easily recorded by a laser beam.

Keeping their work aligned by a laser, machinists can tell if the objects they are shaping change position by less than one hundredth of an inch. One laser company makes instruments that measures silicone wafers for the semiconductor circuits in a computer. Printing ever more complex circuits on ever smaller wafers requires them to be flat within one ten-thousandth of an inch. This would not have been possible before lasers came into being.

Measuring in Space and on Earth

Lasers can also measure distances in outer space. For the first time, we know exactly how far we are away from the Moon at different times of the year.

A laser has been aimed at the surface of the Moon to bounce back from a reflector left on its surface by our astronauts. By keeping track of how long it takes the beam to return to Earth, we can translate time to miles. By knowing that light travels at 182,282 miles (293,474 kilometers) per second, we now know that the closest we are ever to the moon is 221,456 miles (356,544 kilometers) and the farthest away is 252,711 miles (406,865 kilometers).

These two laser beams, at the Observatory of the Côte d'Azur, France, are measuring distances in space. The horizontal beam measures the distance from the Earth to the Moon, with an accuracy to within 1.2 inches (three centimeters). The vertical beam measures the distance to Earth-orbiting satellites.

Today's land surveyors are rarely without a laser measuring device. Unlike the strings and tapes used a few years ago to mark out the building boundaries, a laser beam is perfectly straight. Imagine the importance of precise measurement when constructing skyscrapers, leveling floors and ceilings, plumbing walls, digging tunnels, laying pipe, and drilling wells.

On some large farms in southern California, a laser beam is being used to level land. A laser beam shot from the cab of a tractor has a sensor that automatically stops the tractor when the beam is interrupted by a bump or a hollow in the ground. A small computer aboard the tractor records the exact place where the beam was broken and adjusts the plow blades up or down to level the ground. It does not take a skilled worker to handle such equipment since the job is preprogrammed.

The Earth Moved

One of the space shuttle's experiments with lasers was designed to measure the planet's movements along fault lines — movements that cause earthquakes. Once every second, the lasers pulsed light to a satellite orbiting six hundred miles (966 kilometers) above. Bounced back to Earth detectors, the lasers revealed that the fault they were studying is moving together faster than anyone thought. Two sides of the deep rift are closing in on each other at the alarming rate of three and one-half inches (8.9 centimeters) a year. Towns on nearly opposite sides of the state of California moved fourteen inches (thirty-five centimeters) closer in four years. In the future, laser measurements may be able to predict when earthquakes are about to occur in time to save lives.

Global Climate Changes

It wasn't long before two scientific instruments — radar and laser — were combined to study weather, resulting in lidar. Similar to the radar that is commonly used to track everything from airplanes in flight to thunderstorms, lidar means *light detection and ranging*.

Lidar can be thought of as optical radar, but instead of bouncing radio waves off its target, it uses short pulses of laser light. Some of the light reflects off tiny particles in the atmosphere called *aerosols*, then back to the telescope aligned with the

A laser beam is fired into the night sky from an observatory on the island of Maui, Hawaii. It is reflected back from a mirror on an Earth-orbiting satellite to provide the first really precise measurements of continental drift. Curving star trails appear because this is a long-exposure photo.

laser. By precisely timing the lidar "echo" and by measuring how much laser light is received by the telescope, scientists can accurately determine the location, distribution, and nature of the particles, from cloud droplets to industrial emissions.

Ice Age or Not?

Is Earth's atmosphere heating up, or will we have another ice age in a few thousand years? Dr. Ed Eloranta and his staff are painting new pictures of the sky. Their High Spectral Resolution Lidar (HSRL) produces direct measurements of the depth of clouds. The very highest are called *cirrus* clouds — thin, fleecy clouds of ice crystals formed into wispy filaments. They can either trap sunlight and warm the air, or in some cases, they shield the Earth from sunlight and keep the climate colder.

A picture-taking apparatus, HSRL, scans the sky in large arcs of very fine light, which build up to create a fan-shaped view of the sky. As the light bounces back after hitting moisture particles or impurities we are putting into the air, the information gathered will help explain the impact of human activity on the atmosphere. A twenty-inch- (fifty-centimeter-) diameter telescope and a complex computer system keeps track of figures that measure the density and composition of clouds. Over a billion numbers an hour are transmitted, proving that only recently could such thorough research be carried out. Computer science has to keep pace with subjects that require such abundant information. No human could graph or file these sources.

What Will Future Figures Show?

It is important to be able to compare figures from one year to another to find out just how much conditions have changed. Are dust particles caused by storms, pollen in the air, or smog from our factories and automobiles?

To find an area free from normal change was difficult, but finally a place was chosen in the middle of our great western prairie. Nebraska was targeted as being satisfactory since there were no large centers of population close by and the land was covered with prairie grasses that had been protected by the government from future farming.

The bulky HSRL equipment was loaded in a large trailer. To stop the equipment being affected by temperature changes, the environment inside was kept as close to a constant as possible. Dr. Ed Eloranta and his staff set up their laboratory. Paivi Piironen, who was working on her Ph.D. thesis, was in charge. She had helped to build the equipment, so if anything went wrong she could help put it back in order. It was possible to move the equipment from one site to another, while scientists from other parts of the country cooperated by taking measurements from other comparative locations.

For four years, this lidar equipment has been taking samples of our atmosphere. While these figures are not conclusive and will have to be monitored much longer, still it seems that even in the purest environment we are treating our atmosphere very poorly. We are finding a lot of pollution up there.

AMAZING FACTS

Lasers were used to align the digging equipment for the undersea tunnel between England and France. Frequently work is started from two different places many miles apart, but when guided by three-dimensional laser techniques, drilling rigs meet exactly as designed. They just aim at the little red dot produced ahead of their drill bit by the laser.

Paivi Piironen

Dr. Paivi Piironen and her husband are both involved in laser research, but at times the direction of their careers has been decided by flipping a coin.

As graduate students attending the University of Joensuu in Finland, there was an opportunity for one representative to attend a conference on lasers to be held in the Soviet Union. Both were in line to be selected. The cost of transportation made it impossible for the two to attend, so the outcome of the dilemma was solved by tossing a coin. Paivi's husband, Antti, won.

Actually it was the logical decision. Paivi was already involved in the construction and assembly of some very important laser equipment the university was planning on using for weather research, the first of its kind in the country.

One doesn't buy laser equipment from a catalog, so constructing is just what she was doing. Piironen admits that she has always enjoyed hands-on work in designing and building "gadgets." These gadgets most frequently involved science projects. If she couldn't find equipment specifically for her purpose, she put on her work gloves, bent glass, soldered pieces, and constructed what was needed.

Neither of her parents worked in the field of science, but that was a subject Piironen always liked, even as a young student. No single professor inspired her to continue along these lines; her curiosity carried her forward in her chosen career. The use of lasers was a relatively new field with many directions open for study.

The next turning point in Piironen's career was decided in a more serious manner than flipping coins. She had applied for grants to continue her research. Word came that she and Antti might be able to fit into a program conducted at the University of Wisconsin in Madison. It would involve the study of climate changes by piercing clouds with laser beams. This new form of technology, called lidar, was just what Piironen was interested in. She was just about to start collecting figures and measurements from the equipment she had designed in Finland. Should she leave friends and family and career to strike out in a new direction? She consulted coworkers in Finland, who encouraged her to accept.

Both Piironen and her husband made the trip to Wisconsin, which she considered at first would be a temporary move. Seven years later, they are happily at work in Madison.

As soon as she arrived, Piironen was put right to work on the university's HSRL equipment. She helped renovate the instrument as it was moved into a huge trailer that would eventually take her to the plains of the Midwest for more research. While working on her Ph.D. thesis, she has become the person most familiar with the equipment. She is busy training other students to take the data she will incorporate into her own work. While Dr. Ed Eloranta spearheaded the HSRL research, Piironen is spending all her hours sorting through the figures to draw a better picture of climate cycles and weather patterns.

She has made trips home to visit family, but Piironen has no second thoughts about returning permanently to Finland. At least not while her work is striking new boundaries.

Paivi Piironen is working on lidar technology at the University of Wisconsin in Madison. Here, the laser beam from a lidar unit scans across the sky to give a two- or three-dimensional map of the pollutant concentration in the air. The chemistry of pollutants may be identified using different laser wavelengths.

A lidar map shows the density of pollution in the air over Albuquerque, New Mexico. The yellow lines are roads and the other colors represent the concentration of pollution in the air, from red (high) through yellow and pale blue to dark blue (low). The worst pollution is over a truck refueling station at a freeway junction.

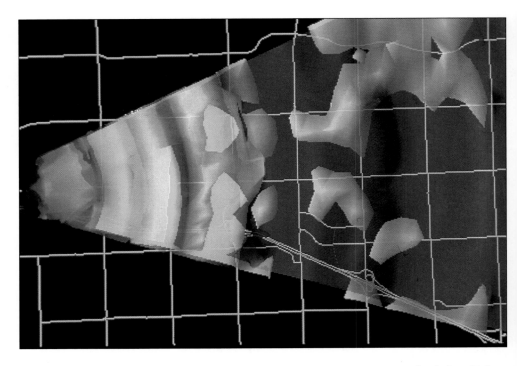

It is hoped by analyzing weather patterns revealed by lidar over a long time, we can predict when certain parts of the world will be suffering from flood or drought. Lidar has been programmed to see through lower layers of clouds to the ceiling of our upper cloud barrier. Accurate pictures can be cataloged. What they will show is of great interest for our future.

Looking Down From the Skies

NASA has tried another approach to scanning the atmosphere. On September 19, 1994, the space shuttle *Discovery* carried a laboratory laser into space. Although only a few hours of data could be collected on this flight, the point of view was a global approach. The space shuttle flew upside down with its cargo bay open toward Earth while the laser system beamed narrow pulses of light through the atmosphere. *Discovery* flew at a relatively low altitude, about 160 miles (250 kilometers), so that the downward-pointing laser pulse was dispersed as little as possible on its way through the atmosphere.

The equipment, named LITE (Lidar In-Space Technology Experiment), used a telescope to measure the laser's light as it was reflected from the clouds, the suspended particles in the air, and the Earth's surface. Engineers will use information from LITE in the development of future instruments, scheduled to begin with satellite launches in 1998.

From its vantage point above the atmosphere, LITE's extremely accurate laser flashes very short pulses of light directly downward, ten times every second. These pulses, lasting less than thirty-billionths of a second, are in three different wavelengths corresponding to ultraviolet, infrared, and visible green light. Because the wavelengths are precisely known and because LITE's telescope is designed to filter out other types of radiation, the signals returning to the shuttle are easy to identify. Timing the returning signals pinpoints the particles' altitude within less than fifteen feet (4.5 meters). By sending out short pulses of laser light and detecting the portion reflected back through the atmosphere, the instrument can obtain a very accurate picture of the atmosphere in distinct slices. These can then be matched to a larger picture that will help us understand our climatic systems.

LITE's science mission takes in a variety of phenomena in widespread geographic areas. Targets include cloud patterns of the western Pacific, cloud decks off the coasts of California and Peru, smoke plumes from fires in South America and Africa, and the direction of desert dust from the Sahara. The science team will study lower atmosphere aerosols over the Amazon rain forest, rock density in the Earth's crust to reveal mining opportunities, and how deserts in the United States, Africa, and China reflect light, which will give information on vegetation. Perhaps the greatest value of early space-based lidars is their accuracy in measuring clouds on a global scale. Information on clouds is critical to improving computer models of global climate.

In a few thousand years, will our descendants be shivering in cold or sweltering in heat? Soon we ought to be able to tell what to expect and prepare for it.

AMAZING FACTS

While the space shuttle was beaming laser rays toward Earth, ground-based laser equipment was aiming toward the same places, so that the LITE data can be compared for accuracy.

AMAZING FACTS

Scientists at NASA told reporters from *Sky* magazine that with all the media hype, "We were reluctant to call the device a laser for fear people would think that with a laser in space, we were going to be zapping everything on the ground. So we're calling it 'Space-Borne Geodynamic Ranging.'"

— Chapter 4 —
Military Uses and Crime Detection

Even when there was only a hint of what lasers could do, the military became very interested in such a concept for a weapon. Perhaps such a gadget could shoot down airplanes, burn holes through tanks, and destroy armies. During the days of the cold war, when the former USSR and the United States were eyeing each other with suspicion, there was a strong fear that satellites, placed in outer space by either country, could beam down destruction.

Between 1962 and 1968, the Army spent some $9 million on laser research but did not come up with any practical, realistic weapons. Small, portable ray guns would require too much energy to produce the beam of fiery heat. Even if such a device could be manufactured, it would be too hot to handle.

Lasers that could shoot down planes seemed more practical. Size would not be too difficult to manage if the weapons were in stationary mounts on the ground. But in the early sixties, the materials used to produce a laser beam were limited. Only a few lasers had been tried, and these had some distinct disadvantages. Researchers tried a mixture of fluorine and hydrogen. These gases produced a lot of power, but individually and together, they had a habit of being very volatile, exploding without warning. The worst result was that the exhaust gas was lethal, killing anyone who breathed it. That was the end of that idea, but no one was ready to give up. There were obvious advantages to a laser weapon if only the right materials could be found.

Weapons in the Field

Military lasers today come in many sizes and shapes. Some can be operated by soldiers in the field. Others are located in high-flying airplanes. And it is believed that a number are in satellites circling the Earth at a height of twenty-two thousand miles (35,420 kilometers).

More recently, the military has tried lasers as actual weapons. In mock battles, lasers have been able to knock out enemy missiles with sighting devices by blinding the equipment. There are also said to be weapons that are strong enough to vaporize everything from thick armor to the delicate electronic systems inside enemy aircraft, tanks, and ships. The United States has experimented with laser beams that have brought down dummy missiles and unpiloted drone planes. Secret research is being carried out, which, it is hoped, will never have to be used.

The Lockheed F-117A Stealth is a modern fighter plane equipped with a laser bomb designator. A laser beam is aimed at a target and a bomb homes in on it. The Stealth fighter has this unusual shape to deflect radar as it flies through enemy territory.

Lasers as Targeting Devices

Recent laser research has not developed a new weapon, but a new device to improve the accuracy of weapons already in use. When firing at a moving target with an ordinary weapon, a bullet must be aimed a bit ahead of the target so that the bullet and target arrive at the same place at the same time. Knowing that gravity pulls a bullet downward, you also have to aim a little above the target.

A laser beam moves at the speed of light, meaning that the beam can travel a mile in one six-millionth of a second. Even if an airplane were traveling at the speed of sound, it would move only about one-sixteenth of an inch while the laser was covering a mile. This is such a small difference that the aim of a weapon does not have to be adjusted. A laser range finder can shoot a beam of light toward a target and immediately calculate the exact time it takes for the shot to reach the target, coming up with the exact distance to the target.

These range finders are small enough to be carried by soldiers in the field or mounted on a tank. When a soldier knows the exact distance to a target, he or she obviously has a much better chance of hitting it.

A laser bomb designator works by shining a low-powered beam at the target. A bomb can be programmed to home in on the laser beam and follow the beam to the target. Once the

Apache helicopters fly over the Saudi Arabian desert. These massive antitank helicopters are equipped with guns, rockets, and sixteen laser-guided missiles. They were very effective in the Gulf War, knocking out key enemy radar sites in Iraq.

target is on the beam, warheads from artillery or missiles from planes that are programmed to see only the laser wavelength can correct their own course, even in flight, and be almost assured of hitting the target.

These smart bombs were used successfully during the Gulf War when the United Nations troops led by forces from the United States were able to hit strategic targets throughout Iraq, cut communications, and disable frontline artillery.

Underwater Communication

Another use of lasers during wartime helped solve the difficulties of communication with submarines in enemy waters. In the past, the only way to get a message to a submarine captain was by radio. Radio waves do not travel well through water, and large antennas are required to broadcast long distances. There is always the chance that an enemy can intercept a message, revealing a sub's location.

The Navy now uses a laser that gives off a beam of blue-green light, which travels well through water. The beam carrying the message is aimed at a satellite high above the ocean. The satellite relays the beam to the sub, which has a special receiver that registers only the blue-green light. In seconds, the beam of light is decoded into a word message by computers.

The satellite flashes the beam for only a few millionths of a second, which would make it almost impossible for the enemy to see it. Even if lookouts have equipment that detects laser light, it has to be tuned to the exact shade of blue-green in the originating beam of light.

Star Wars

In the mid-1980s, President Ronald Reagan launched a huge military research program called Strategic Defense Initiative (SDI), nicknamed "Star Wars" after the science fiction movie of that

A long time ago, science fiction suggested that ray guns might beam down destruction from space, and the movie Star Wars *further popularized such ideas. In this modern artist's impression, a laser is being fired at a target satellite from a space shuttle's payload bay.*

name. The idea was to mount laser sensors on satellites that would detect incoming missiles. The missiles would then be shot out of the sky before they could strike American targets.

The U.S. military is also searching for defensive systems that will guard against enemy lasers. One way is to cover possible targets with reflective material that will bounce back an incoming laser beam. Another idea is to protect a target by blanketing it with many thin layers of material to fool the message being sent back to the enemy. An even more complicated process is to have the surface layer of the target spinning around, so that the laser spreads out over a larger area.

Matching Fingerprints

While the military is trying to protect the country from attack, local law enforcement personnel are trying to protect individuals from crime. Detectives have long used fingerprinting to track down criminals, but the sheer volume of records is mind-boggling.

Six years after the murder of Miriam Slamovich, a forty-six-year old woman who was shot during a burglary attempt, the police still hadn't found a suspect. Plenty of evidence had been left behind. Fingerprints had been lifted from door and window sills. Over three hundred thousand prints had been examined over the six-year period. None had been matched.

In 1984, the break came. The San Francisco police department had installed one of the country's finest automatic fingerprint identification systems (AFIS). The computer came up with a short list of suspects. Eventually, one of these suspects confessed to the killing.

Today, that list would have been narrowed to a single suspect. A beam of laser light scans the prints, either from file records or from the crime scene. This information is fed into a computer, which produces a map of the ridge patterns of each print. The map is translated into a digital (numerical) code and stored in the memory of the computer. Not only can this information be used for local files of prints, they can be compared with prints in the international registry kept by the FBI office in Washington, D.C.

One of the most amazing cases cracked by laser equipment occurred in the trial of a former Nazi, a Rumanian Orthodox priest named Trifia. He was being deported because it was said that he had falsified information about his background. He denied any knowledge of past connections with the Nazis.

The West German government then supplied the FBI with a number of documents, including a postcard Trifia had allegedly written in 1942 to Heinrich Himmler, of the Nazi secret police. Trifia, of course, denied that he had ever written the card.

The FBI decided to try a new technique using a laser. The beam of light was aimed at the postal card. Even after forty-two years, the laser was able to pick up traces of perspiration and body oil that were made when the Trifia handled the object. That residue absorbed the single wavelength light of the laser and glowed with a light different from the laser's. It reradiated the laser's light, or played it back, at longer wavelengths. By observing an illuminated specimen through a filter that excluded all wavelengths that would normally be seen with the naked eye, technicians were able to detect even the faintest trace of human contact, proving the card had been written by Trifia. He was returned to his native country where he stood trial, was convicted, and imprisoned.

From military defense to a courtroom defense based on fingerprints, lasers can help protect countries and individuals.

Roland L. Menzel

Dr. Menzel has been called on by more than one hundred law enforcement agencies in this country and abroad to study fingerprint evidence, helping to catch criminals who had long escaped detection. With only the most minute evidence, he has been able to identify culprits even years after the crime was committed.

All this has been possible through the ever-growing improvement in laser technology, some involving Dr. Menzel's own experiments with different types of lasers. When these lasers hit an object, it glows with a different colored light than that of the laser. You can see a similar phenomenon when a black light, which emits invisible light, is shone onto a white shirt; the shirt fluoresces, or gives off a light.

In addition to his expert knowledge on fingerprint detection, Menzel has developed procedures to diagnose dental problems using a laser beam. He has also been involved in improving methods of etching computer chips that are read with laser beams. In Saudi Arabia he has been asked to prospect for oil and gas by sensing methane gas with laser beams. He has also used lasers to detect any breaks in cable insulation and sensitive sealing caps under pressure.

Roland Menzel was born June 14, 1943, in Linz, Austria. He attended primary school in Germany and later in Brazil, where his family emigrated. Even with a radical change in language and culture, young Menzel showed a remarkable ability to adapt and maintain excellent grades in school.

(Below) The picture on the left is an unsuccessful attempt to make a fingerprint visible by a widely used chemical process. The other picture shows how laser examination made the fingerprint clearly visible.

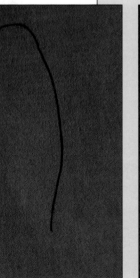

He had already decided to come to the United States for further study, and in 1963, he enrolled at Glendale College in California. In his senior year, Menzel transferred to the University of California in Los Angeles, but that was just the beginning. He received his Ph.D. degree from Washington State University, where he specialized in a field of physics where substances are studied through a laser spectroscope. This instrument breaks down the components of a substance by studying the lines of color and widths of color, accurately identifying gases and telling something of the properties they possess. Each gas carries its own signature.

One of Roland Menzel's students at Texas Technical University using a laser in the laboratory.

As time went on, Menzel turned to teaching, introducing many young students to the excitement of new techniques and areas for experimentation. He has taught chemistry at Purdue University where he was engaged in research with the use of laser spectroscopy, studying how energy is transferred during the growing cycle of plants. His knowledge of lasers was also used in studying complex metal structures when he was on the faculty of the University of Kentucky. Director for forensic studies, he is presently head of the physics department of Texas Technical University in Lubbock, Texas, where he has been an honored member of the faculty since 1983. He is also a member of the scientific staff of the Xerox Research Center in Canada.

Roland Menzel has traveled the world, and the world has come to him for answers.

— Chapter 5 —
Pictures That
Seem Real

Making a hologram of a statuette. A beam of laser light is split in two, part of the beam illuminating the subject before striking a photosensitive glass plate, the other part striking the plate directly.

One of the most amazing applications of laser science is the hologram, what seems to be a three-dimensional picture shown on a flat surface. Holography, the art of making holograms, comes from the Greek words *holos*, meaning whole, and *graphos*, meaning picture.

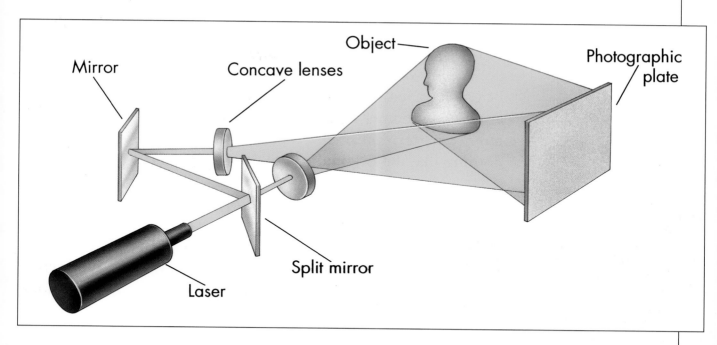

Searching for a way to sharpen pictures of very tiny objects taken with an electron microscope, Dennis Gabor discovered the principle of holography as early as 1947, long before the laser came into being. He came up with a fuzzy — but startling — image. It seemed to jump forward from the photographic plate as if it were a real image in three dimensions. Perfecting the idea was not possible until a coherent beam of light, one that was all of one wavelength, was available. But the theory of holography started people experimenting with the techniques Dennis Gabor had invented.

To make a hologram today, a laser beam is aimed at a partially silvered mirror, called a split mirror that divides the light into two distinct beams. One beam is reflected by a mirror on to the object to be photographed. This is called the object beam. The other is reflected directly on the photographic plate. This is called the reference beam.

When the object beam of the laser bounces off the item to be photographed, it showers the film with light from all angles of the object upon which it is focused. The reference beam is really a blank beam focusing only on a blank photographic plate. When

Laser light is split so that some of it hits an object and is reflected onto a photographic plate while the rest shines directly at the same plate. This light from different angles creates an interference pattern that spectators see as a change of perspective when they look at the hologram from different points.

the two beams meet on the film, they create an interference pattern. This means the waves of light clash and mesh.

When wavelengths of the same size meet, they create a brighter image. If the crest of one wave meets the trough of another, a dimmer image is produced. The record of this interference pattern on photographic film is the hologram. It looks nothing like the original object, but it contains all the information needed to reproduce the light that originally came from the object. If you tip the finished film from side to side what you see is apparently a change of perspective. It's almost as if you are seeing around an object.

A boy stands in front of a hologram at the Palace of Discovery in Paris. This is a reflection hologram made on sheet film and illuminated by a halogen lamp.

Many Uses for Holograms

Commercially, holograms have been reproduced on objects ranging from credit cards and jewelry to magazine and book covers. The United States Postal Service even used one on a commemorative stamp. They are made out of thin sheets of aluminum-coated plastic with very fine ridges built in. It is these ridges that allow you to see the changing images of the hologram. What we see as round and real is actually light reflected from the objects from more than one angle.

Holograms can also be used to discover defects in manufactured items. A hologram is made of a perfect specimen, for example, a

propeller. On top of the original, another hologram is made of the propeller to be tested. If there is a defect in the manufactured item when the two holograms are superimposed, the light waves will produce an interference pattern, which will show up any defect. This way manufacturers can test their products without tearing them apart, helping engineers find small stress lines in a solid object.

Military uses for holograms are almost within our grasp. The Air Force is designing a cockpit with hologram projections of instrument panels beamed on to the canopy of the plane so that pilots would not have to look down at the instrument panel when in the midst of battle.

Scientists are most interested in using holographs in computer information storage and retrieval systems. Researchers are developing multilaser chips that are capable of storing up to one trillion bits of information, more than either magnetic tape or microfilm. There has also been research on a three-dimensional "cube" memory based on holography. Many miraculous uses are ahead for this new science.

AMAZING FACTS

X-ray holography of cells within the body is being perfected so that doctors can get a better three-dimensional view of the inside of the body.

Dennis Gabor (1900–1979)

Dennis Gabor was born in Budapest, Hungary, on June 5, 1900. A great deal of his early work and interest in science occurred in Germany, where he had gone to get the finest education available at the time. He was a promising student, with the ability to concentrate his energy without giving up on complicated projects.

Gabor seemed to thrive on difficulty, never choosing a road well traveled. It was always a challenge that caught his eye. He received his first degree and doctorate at the Technical University of Berlin. He was asked to stay on as a professor, but that would have meant giving up his time researching new fields. Instead, Gabor began his career as an industrial research engineer in Berlin, Germany. Teaching was to come later.

Already, it was evident that Nazi Germany, under the leadership of Adolf Hitler, was turning into a police state. Many of his colleagues were content with their lives, but Gabor could see what direction his life might take if he stayed on. The type of courses to be offered at the Technical University were being limited to what certain government officials thought would be of use to Germany in case of war. Gabor's interests were more along the lines of theoretical mathematics and the analysis of the smallest specks of matter. This was not a very practical field of study according to those who were running the institution.

As more and more of his freedoms were taken away from him, Gabor decided to leave the country forever. He had made contact with some fellow scientists in Britain over the years of his study. Now seemed to be an appropriate time to make discreet inquiries about continuing his research in London. It was at the Imperial College of Science and Technology that he continued his work in applied electronic physics.

Gabor was very interested in the electron microscope, which was a great improvement over the very best light microscopes of the day. The best magnification possible with a light microscope could be compared to taking pictures of a raindrop rather than to the microscopic particles contained in that raindrop.

What he set about doing was to take a bad electron picture, but one that contained the whole information, and correct it by optical (light) means. This was the very heart of the theory of holograms, taking a picture of an object and have it meet a beam of light that was aimed at a blank surface, so that the interference would bring up a picture in three dimensions.

Mathematics proved that the principle was right, but this was before anyone had been able to make a laser light all of one wavelength. In order to achieve even an imperfect three-dimensional image, Gabor had to illuminate an object with a high-pressure mercury lamp through a pinhole. The disturbance on the picture came about because the two beams were not exactly alike. He continued to work on these principles, making it possible to see individual atoms with the electron microscope.

Dennis Gabor with a holographic image of himself.

Gabor began teaching in 1949, with the hope that he could interest some of his students to continue the search for the perfect answer, and wrote several books and papers that covered a much broader field. He became internationally known for his work in many fields of physics and received dozens of awards.

In later life, Gabor came to the United States to take the position of staff scientist at CBS Laboratories in Stamford, Connecticut. But he returned to London, which he really considered his home. It was here that he died February 8, 1979.

— Chapter 6 —
Lasers and Communication

In the 1960s, the laser was called a solution looking for a problem. Today, you can hardly find a field where they are not in use. One of the most important jobs for lasers is in the field of communication, sending information through very thin glass fibers. This system is called *fiber optics*.

It would not have been possible without the work of an inventor named Norman R. French. In 1934, he proposed taking a hollow pipe and lining it with reflective material. A light shined into one end would travel through the pipe, turning corners and going wherever the pipe led. However, French was not attempting to send information but trying to send light from one room to another without wires.

Thirty-five years later, his idea was given a different twist. In 1970, Robert Maurer of the Corning Glass Works in Corning, New York, constructed the first long-distance optical fiber. The fiber is only a fraction of an inch in diameter and consists of a central core and cladding around the outside. The cladding on the outside makes the inside edge of the

The optical fibers shown here are from a domestic lamp, with a human hand to show the size. Optical fibers carry laser light patterns, even bending the light around corners. When sound is turned into laser light, messages can be sent around the world.

cladding of the fiber reflective, forcing the light photons to bounce back into the core. While laser beams of light can only produce light in a straight line, the optical fiber can bend light and carry it around corners. As long as the curves are not too sharp, the photon beam hits the cladding at an angle, then continues on.

A few photons do get through the cladding and eventually weaken the beam, so it is necessary to have small stations set up at intervals to boost the signals. Today, some optical fibers carry light more than twenty-six miles (forty kilometers) before the signal has to be amplified.

A Code That Carries Information

Light can carry information in two different ways. An analog system provides for an infinite number of levels of brightness, ranging from completely off to totally on. So, in an analog format, sound waves can be translated into light waves of varying brightness. The other system, called the *digital format*, has only two levels — on or off. A digital system translates the information from sound waves into a pattern of very short, very fast bursts of light, almost as if the sender were using the old-fashioned way of using dots and dashes of Morse Code through an electrical wire.

The quick pulses of light are a code for the original sound wave form of the spoken word. When you use your home telephone, the equipment changes the vibration of your voice into electric current that copies the pattern of sound waves. The sound must then be turned from an analog signal into a digital signal. The digital flow of electricity is then sent to the laser. The laser sends out a light pattern that follows the pattern of the electric flow.

The light speeds through the glass filament at over one hundred thousand miles (161,000 kilometers) per second to the phone at the other end of the line. Here, the light pattern strikes a photodetector, which changes it back into electricity and, in turn, into sound.

AMAZING FACTS

Most of the telephone links between major cities are now made with optical fibers, using lasers smaller than a pinhead as the source of the signals transmitting the information.

AMAZING FACTS

The light in the fiber of a typical telephone system switches on and off several million times a second.

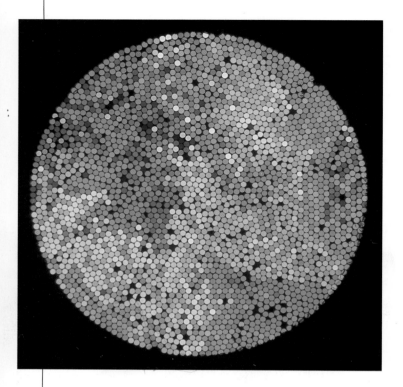

A magnified cross section of a glass fiber optic cable showing the illuminated tips of the individual strands. This sort of cable, made of pure quartz, is used for the transatlantic telephone sytem. Many thousands of phone calls can be carried simultaneously as beams of laser light.

These fibers are unbelievably thin, five one-thousandths of an inch thick, almost half the diameter of a human hair. In spite of its delicacy, each fiber has been tested to have twice the strength of steel, being able to withstand a pull of six hundred thousand pounds per square inch (42,180 kilograms per square centimeter).

Advantages of Laser Optics

One of the benefits of laser optics is that several fibers can be packaged in one cable. One hundred and forty-four glass fibers can be contained in a single cable that is smaller than your little finger. This one cable can carry over fifty thousand messages at once.

A cable this size is joined with others like it. Fiber optic cables today can carry several hundreds of thousands of conversations at one time. They can do this because beams of light do not interfere with each other, so there is no noise in the system. When metal wires are packed closely together, the separate signals interfere with each other and produce electrical noise. Another advantage is that glass fibers transmit messages at very high speeds. In addition, if anyone tries to tap into a line, it breaks the filament and destroys the signal, so it's difficult to "wiretap" or spy on someone. However, with the right equipment, you can pick up the stray light on the outside of the fiber and understand a conversation.

Lasers in the Supermarket

Of all laser uses, probably the most common is the bar code label reader at supermarket checkout counters. As the clerk slides a can of soup or a box of cereal over an opening, a laser light wraps around the item, so that the message can be read anywhere up to 180 degrees from the scanning window, not just on the flat surface of the bottom of a box or can. Each item bears a series of parallel lines, the Universal Product Code (UPC). Coded in these stripes is the name of the manufacturer, a description of the product, and its weight. The laser beam bounces off the UPC and strikes a receiver within the counter. The receiver causes the beeper to sound and also signals a computer. The computer memory finds the price, shows it on the screen, and prints it out on the paper tape that becomes the receipt. A low-powered inexpensive laser is used so that there is no danger of causing harm to eyes.

A fan of laser light at a pop festival. Exciting new laser effects, using special mirrors, projectors, and prisms, are being devised all the time for films and the entertainment industry.

Light Shows

Laser light shows have accompanied rock bands, symphony orchestras, productions of *Peter Pan,* and all kinds of theatrical spectaculars, painting pictures in the sky, flashing ribbons of color overhead. Laser light is beamed in a straight line, of course, but it can be focused through prisms, scanners, and oscillators. It can be translated from sharp spikes of color to gauzy, underwater dream shapes.

Bounce mirrors hung above an audience can create other effects, making one beam appear to be many. A special scanning projector can twist the light into intricate patterns resulting in swirling figures. This growing art form often forms an integral part of many musical and theatrical productions.

A laser beam is reflected off an audio CD's surface, making a multicolored interference pattern. A CD stores music as a series of fine depressions. This layer is coated with a fine metal film that follows these depressions exactly and reflects the laser light. On top is a layer of clear plastic.

AMAZING FACTS

A CD-ROM can hold 650 megabytes of information — enough for over sixty-five thousand pages of text.

Compact Discs or CDs

Until the 1980s, sound could be permanently recorded in only two ways. One was with grooves on a flat round record. The other was with a tape containing a pattern of magnetized metal particles. Since 1983, a greatly improved method of recording has come into being with the use of the laser. Sound can now be recorded on microscopic flat spots and dips arranged in a spiral on a small flat disc. Such a recording is known as a CD or compact disc.

A laser beam shines on the disc from below. A photodetector, also under the CD, senses the difference between light reflected from a flat spot and light reflected from a tiny pit. The machine then changes this pattern back into sound, and the listener can hear music.

The disc has a protective plastic coating. As only light is touching it, not a phonograph needle, a CD can last a lot longer, although the pit pattern on the disk will eventually degrade. Plus, CDs provide a very realistic sound.

Other CDs are read by computers and carry information, sound, and pictures. These CD-ROMs (Read Only Memory) can carry vast amounts of information. Today, a CD for your computer can record all twenty-three volumes of an encyclopedia on one disc.

While we may still think of lasers as purely for science and industry, they are entering our homes almost secretly. Telephone conversations across many miles boosted by fiber optics and lush music more true-to-life than ever before are all made commonplace by lasers.

Chapter 7
Lasers Today and Tomorrow

Lasers can do amazing things. A diamond is the hardest natural material on Earth. To produce copper wire, soft copper metal is forced through a small hole in a diamond. The diamond acts as a mold. It used to take two days to pierce a diamond by hand. Today, a gem can be cut in seconds with a few blasts from a high-energy laser. Yet lasers can also put pin-sized openings in soft baby bottle nipples.

A laser is also much more accurate than a mechanical drill. In one demonstration, a laser was able to put two hundred holes in the head of an ordinary sewing pin. Since a laser never touches the object it is working on, there is no danger that it could jar it out of line.

A laser, mounted on a robot arm, cuts through a metal plate. Lasers are more accurate than other cutting methods, and they can easily cut through the hardest materials.

Lasers are used to weld metal parts together. With a laser beam, only a small amount of heat is transferred to the parts to be welded. This reduces the possibility of the metal being warped or distorted with extreme heat. Pinhead-sized transistors that need three exactly polished welds can be put together by lasers that bond one-millimeter (.04-inch) wires in a millionth of a second.

The Navy uses huge lasers to cut and weld steel sections of ships, and a manufacturer of men's suits may use a laser to cut through one hundred layers of fabric, never varying its measurements. Laser engravings on wood, plastic, or metal are commonplace.

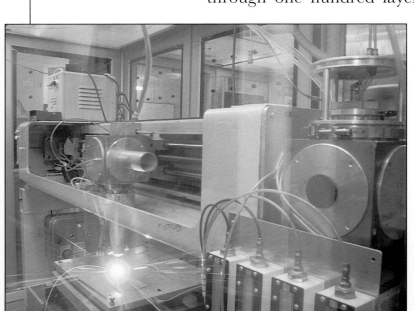

A carbon dioxide laser is used for welding. Lasers are essential for precise welding of objects of all sizes and for jobs where metal might be warped by the heat produced by other methods.

Lasers come in all sizes, some using crystals as a medium, like Theodore Maiman's first ruby laser, others using gases or liquids. Some lasers may cost as much as $500,000, but they have proved to be profitable because of the time saved and the accuracy mastered. General Motors, America's largest automobile manufacturer, hardens the metal housings of power steering mechanisms with seventeen lasers that cost two million dollars. When combined with computer-controlled systems, lasers can operate completely automatically.

Laser printers can print up to forty-five thousand characters a second. Color photographs reproduce faithfully when scanned by specially designed lasers. Laser engraving systems work by vaporizing bits of a rubber roller to match the pattern of light and dark in the artwork, leaving a raised image that's used to print the image on paper.

Preserving Works of Art

When Dr. John Asmus went to Venice, Italy, to make holographic records of the city's famous statuary in the late 1970s, he made a discovery. The black crust on the white marble statues, caused by years of air pollution and salt water breezes, flooding, and pigeon droppings, burned away under the laser's hot beam. The marble underneath did not absorb the laser's energy and remained unharmed. Asmus was also called upon to restore some irreplaceable Indian rock paintings in Utah that vandals had attempted to destroy.

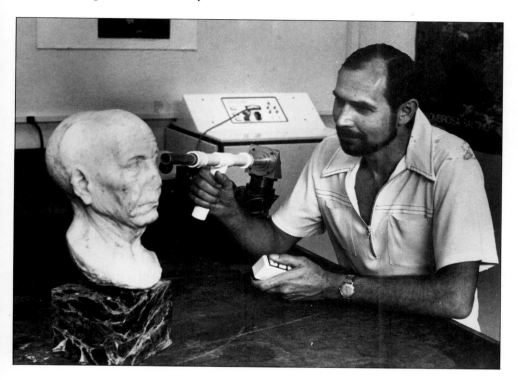

Dr. John Asmus tests a new laser technique for vaporizing grime and encrustations from old stonework. It takes only a fraction of the time of other cleaning methods and there is no risk of harming valuable historical objects.

Nuclear Power

The nuclear forces that hold atoms and their parts together are the strongest known. The Sun is always generating great amounts of energy. The heat from the Sun is so great that some of the hydrogen atoms it contains are forced together. They combine to become larger atoms of the element helium. This process is called fusion. Scientists have tried to copy this process, the basis of the superpowerful hydrogen bomb.

The center for laser-fusion research is at the Lawrence Livermore National Laboratory in Livermore, California. Scientists there have built the most powerful laser in the world, called Nova. It can deliver up to one hundred trillion watts of power.

Gary Sterken

By the time Gary Sterken first chose to be a doctor, he had heard of experimental laser surgery. Here was an exciting, entirely new concept. It would take a lot of study and research before safety requirements would be met. No one wanted to think of a beam of light strong enough to vaporize tissue aimed at their eyes.

As a young boy living on a dairy farm in southern Wisconsin, Gary Sterken never started out to be a doctor. Medical school seemed like a long and difficult way off. But he was a good student, who applied himself well in any undertaking, no matter how hard, and patient almost to a fault.

Just to complete four years of undergraduate work at Lawrence University put him in serious debt. Instead of choosing biological science, which seemed crowded with many would-be doctors, he decided on chemistry as his major so he could find a job after graduation.

Four days after receiving his diploma, Sterken was at work at the State Crime Lab, where he worked until his student loan was paid off. Even at this time, he was working with laser technology, not on human tissue, but on inanimate objects that could reveal secrets when bombarded with seemingly magical beams of light energy.

Then it was back to school for his medical degree and nine hard years of work before he became a practicing surgeon. Eye surgery fascinated him, and for the first time, he became aware of the possibilities the new use of lasers offered.

First, doctors were trained for the delicate work using corpses. Then, living animals were used and finally humans who were in such need of treatment that their sight would be lost if help was not available. More and more successes were reported, and more and more new techniques were developed for other complicated cases of eye abnormalities.

Doctors were now able to actually reshape the lens of a person's eye. At first, small cuts had been made around the cornea, so that in healing, the curve could be changed. This required the most delicate work. Today, with expensive new equipment,

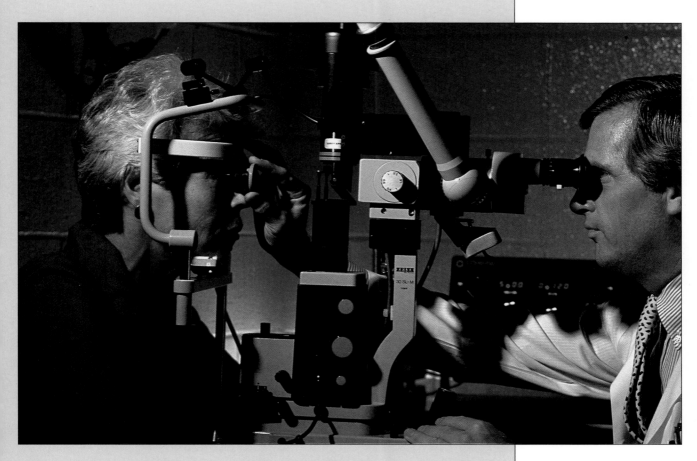

patience and precision, doctors are able to shave off minute layers of the cornea with this excimer surgery. Most ophthalmologists have the opportunity to use small lasers in their practice. But for excimer surgery, only the most advanced lasers are used, lasers that cost $500,000 to purchase and at least $100,000 to maintain. This is a small price to pay, says Dr. Sterken, for a machine that can bring help to hundreds. Think of the number of people who suffer from nearsightedness. With excimer surgery, they can throw their glasses away forever. This may not be possible for everyone, but for many, it is a miraculous cure.

Before his retirement in the distant future, Sterken is sure there will be new miracles to perform. Most will depend on new ways to use laser techniques that can mend blood vessels, shrink tissue, and actually drill holes in eyes painlessly to restore sight. The future of vision will be shaped by people like Gary Sterken.

An ophthalmologist about to undertake laser eye surgery makes adjustments to a focusing laser to ensure correct alignment before using the main beam.

A single laser beam is divided into ten separate beams. These are aimed through 460-foot- (140-meter-) long tubes where they are further amplified. Then, all ten beams are aimed at a 16-foot- (5-meter-) wide aluminum chamber. At the center of the chamber is a tiny pellet about the size of a grain of sand, which contains the hydrogen. The beams zap this small speck for a fraction of a second, bringing its temperature up to nearly five million degrees Fahrenheit. At this temperature, the atoms fuse, sending forth a burst of energy.

The fusion process relies on blasting the tiny fuel pellet to raise the temperature so quickly that the fusion reaction occurs. The primary difficulty is that the huge machines pump in more energy to create fusion than is returned by the nuclear reaction. But some day in the not too distant future, scientists hope to solve that major problem. If it would be possible to control this great power, we would have all the energy the world would ever need.

Lasers can enrich the uranium used as nuclear fuel. There are two types of uranium. Power stations need large quantities of the rare uranium-235, which is found with the more common uranium-238. The laser ionizes atoms of uranium-235, which are then attracted to an electrode so the gas around the electrode will be richer in uranium-235.

The Future of Lasers

Dr. John D. Rather, who has been working in the field of lasers since their beginning, says that he feels in time, "Lasers will change the world as much as the invention of electricity."

Medical doctors have been developing their use of lasers for delicate surgery never before attempted. Brain surgery to correct abnormalities, even in new-born infants, is even now a possibility. Lasers have been developed that can pass through normal tissues and destroy only what has been targeted for removal.

As the speed of light is the fastest rate at which information can be sent, computers are bound to use optical (light) signals as their capacity to store information increases. Eventually, lasers and optical fibers will almost completely replace electronic circuits.

Storing information with the same technique used in making holograms means that a hundred times more data can be processed and held for future use in a compact space than was ever possible before. With scientists needing more and more figures to design everything from miniature circuits to space-traveling rockets, lasers will be a necessity.

The future of holograms themselves seems limitless. Picture yourself at home watching a three-dimensional movie on your television screen. Holograms may also be used in virtual reality pictures, both for wide-screen television viewing and telephone communication. You may be able to talk to someone on the telephone while seeming to view that person right in your own room. Important conferences could be handled this way.

All of this has happened within the last forty years. No wonder the world is looking for even more dramatic breakthroughs in the field of laser technology. Natural resources such as coal, oil, and wood will be saved for other uses. We may even be able to clear the air of pollutants. What other invention could have so much potential for good?

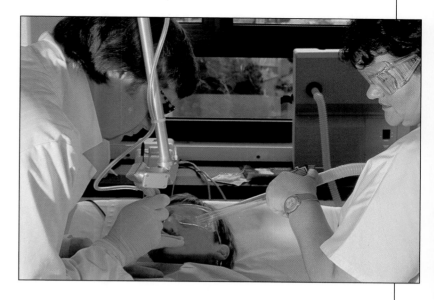

Laser surgery can remove skin blemishes such as birthmarks and tattoos. Many types of surgical lasers have been designed to give a variety of effects on human tissues.

AMAZING FACTS

Albert Einstein, the great physicist, predicted the possibility of lasers in 1917. He said one could stimulate the emission of electromagnetic radiation in an object by stimulating the electrons of the atoms in the object. The amplification would generate a beam with a uniform wavelength and particles moving in the same direction — in other words, a laser.

Timeline

1800 — German physicist Max Planck discovers small particles of light, naming them photons.

1917 — Albert Einstein proposes the theory of spontaneous emission.

1934 — Norman French develops the first hollow glass pipe through which light can pass and be directed around curves. This was the forerunner of optical fibers.

1947 — Dennis Gabor discovered the basic principles of holography.

1954 — Charles Hard Townes demonstrates the maser.

1960 — Theodore Harold Maiman makes the first ruby laser.

1962 — First laser surgery on humans.

Late 1960s — Soviet professor Youri Denisyouk applies holography to the reproduction of artworks.

1970 — First long-distance optical fibers produced by Robert Maurer.

1971 — Dennis Gabor wins the Nobel Prize in physics for his invention and development of the holographic method.

1972 — Experimental laser bomb designator is developed.

1986 — With a combination of holography and computers, a team from the Massachusetts Institute of Technology manages to represent a car in three dimensions. This technique can help reduce the time it takes to design a car.

1994 — Lidar, a type of laser equipment, studies the atmosphere from the space shuttle in flight.

Further Reading

Asimov, Isaac. *How Did We Find Out About Lasers?* New York: Walker and Company, 1970

Berger, Melvin. *Lights, Lenses, and Lasers.* New York: G. P. Putnam's Sons, 1987.

Carroll, John Millar. *The Story of the Laser.* New York: Dutton Publishers, 1964.

Eskow, Dennis. *Laser Careers.* New York: Franklin Watts, 1988.

Flatow, Ira. *They All Laughed.* New York: Harper Collins Publishers, 1993.

Kettlekamp, Larry. *Lasers, The Magic Light.* New York: Dodd, Mead & Company, 1979.

Lawrence, Clifford L. *The Laser Book.* New York: Prentice Hall Press, 1986.

Mauer, Allan. *Lasers, Light Wave of the Future.* New York: Arco Publishers, Inc., 1982.

Taylor, J. R., and P. M. W. French. *How Lasers Are Made.* New York: Facts On File Publications, 1987.

Glossary

Aerosol: Particles held in suspension in the air.

Amplification: The process of making something bigger, more powerful.

Amplitude: A measurement of the height of light wave from its crest or trough to a center line.

Atom: The smallest unit of a chemical element.

Electron: An electrically charged particle circling the nucleus of an atom. The charge is negative

Emission: Something that is sent off or given off, especially something that is discharged into the air.

Frequency: A measurement of the number of waves of light that pass a given point during a certain length of time.

Fluorescence: Giving off light as long as the item is exposed to specific rays of energy, such as ultraviolet rays of light.

Joule: One watt of power radiated for one second.

Laser: A machine that makes a very strong beam of light. *Laser* stands for the phrase *l*ight *a*mplification by *s*timulated *e*mission of *r*adiation.

Laser bomb designator: Measures the distance from a weapon to its target by using a laser.

Lidar: Optical radar that uses light waves instead of radio waves to detect an object.

Microwaves: Electromagnetic waves of extremely high frequency.

Optical fiber: A thin filament through which light can pass.

Patent: A permit issued by the government that allows an inventor the sole right to make, use, and sell his or her invention for a specified period of time. Depending on the invention, patents can be worth millions of dollars.

Photon: A unit of light energy.

Radiation: Energy that is transmitted in the form of rays, waves, or particles.

Watt: A measurement of the brightness of light.

Index

Numbers in *italic* indicate pictures; numbers in **bold** indicate biographies